MEET THE GREATS

William SHAKESPEARE

TIM COOKE

Gareth Stevens PUBLISHING

Please visit our website, **www.garethstevens.com**.
For a free color catalog of all our high-quality books,
call toll free 1-800-542-2595 or fax 1-877-542-2596.

CATALOGING-IN-PUBLICATION DATA

Names: Cooke, Tim.
Title: William Shakespeare / Tim Cooke.
Description: New York : Gareth Stevens, 2017. | Series: Meet the greats | Includes index.
Identifiers: ISBN 9781482459647 (pbk.) | ISBN 9781482459661 (library bound) | ISBN 9781482459654 (6 pack)
Subjects: LCSH: Shakespeare, William, 1564-1616--Juvenile literature. | Dramatists, English--Early modern, 1500-1700--Biography--Juvenile literature.
Classification: LCC PR2895.C66 2017 | DDC 822.3'3--dc23

Published in 2017 by
Gareth Stevens Publishing
111 East 14th Street, Suite 349
New York, NY 10003

For Brown Bear Books Ltd:
Editorial Director: Lindsey Lowe
Managing Editor: Tim Cooke
Children's Publisher: Anne O'Daly
Design Manager: Keith Davis
Designer and illustrator: Supriya Sahai
Picture Manager: Sophie Mortimer

Concept development: Square and Circus / Brown Bear Books Ltd

Picture Credits: Front Cover: Character artwork, Supriya Sahai. Interior: KB National Library of the Netherlands: 10b; e venise: 36; Metropolitan Museum of Art: 9; Public Domain: thinlink/engelshitoria/duna/RHL 13; Shutterstock: AnersPhoto 42b, Arena Photo UK 43, George Kollidas 21, Peter Turner Photography 8t; Thinkstock: Bycostello Photography 30, Dorling Kindersley 15, istockphoto 34, 38t, 40, George Kollidas 38b, Photos.com 19, 23, 28, 29, 31; Wellcome Images: 22t; Westminster Abbey: 39; Wikipedia: Elliot Brown 10, Corpus Christi College, Cambridge 20, Dulwich Picture Gallery 24, Folger Education 14, 22b, Folger Shakespeare Library 35t, Topham Forrest 32, Tony Hisgett 33, Illustrated London News 25t, PD/RHL 25b, J. Schneider 12, Sotherby's New York 41, Tulane Public Relations 11, Johannes de Witt 18, Yale University: Beinecke Rare Book & Manuscript Library 42t, Searching for Shakespeare/Tanya Cooper/YUP 25br.

Printed in the United States of America
CPSIA compliance information: Batch CW17GS: For further information contact Gareth Stevens, New York, New York at 1-800-542-2595.

Contents

Introduction

William Shakespeare wrote some of the most famous plays ever written. They are still popular today.

William Shakespeare (1564–1616) is the most famous **playwright** in the world. Even though it is 400 years since Shakespeare died, at least one of his plays is being performed every day somewhere in the world. The plays have been translated from English into more than 75 languages. They have been turned into comic books, movies, musicals, ballets, and puppet shows. There are Shakespeare theater companies and Shakespeare festivals all around the world.

Shakespeare wrote 37 plays and 154 poems known as **sonnets**, but we know very little about him as a man. There are no records about much of his life. Some people believe that Shakespeare did not even write the plays for which he is famous. But for most people, Shakespeare expressed ideas about how people behave toward each other that are as true today as they were 400 years ago.

Obscure BEGINNINGS

There were no signs in William's early life that he would grow up to be one of the greatest of all writers.

We know very little about Shakespeare's early life. For example, no one knows his exact birthdate in 1564. It is usually said to be April 23, which is St. George's Day. St. George is the **patron saint** of England. Church records note that Shakespeare was baptized on April 26, 1564. Babies in Elizabethan England were usually baptized three days after their birth. We do know for sure that William was born in Stratford-upon-Avon, which is a small town in Warwickshire in central England. Stratford was a quiet, rural place where many people were farmers.

QUICK FACTS

- No one knows William's real birthday.
- After leaving school, at age 14, most boys like William went to university. William did not!

William was born in the house on the left of this photograph.

SHAKESPEARE'S FAMILY

William was the third of eight children born to Mary and John Shakespeare. His mother, Mary Arden, was the daughter of a wealthy landowner. William had two older sisters, but they died when they were still babies. Soon after William's birth, **plague** reached Stratford. The disease killed 200 people in the town, but William survived. Mary and John Shakespeare had another five children after William. The youngest, Edmund, was born in 1580. By that time, William was 16 years old. As the oldest child, William would have been expected to help with his brothers and sisters at home and to set a good example for them.

AN IMPORTANT FAMILY

John Shakespeare was a glove maker. That was an important job in Elizabethan England. John was successful and bought property and houses in Stratford. In 1568, when William was four years old, John was elected as mayor of Stratford for a year. He held other positions in the town government over the next 20 years. Around the start of 1577, however, John's business began to decline and by the 1580s he was in debt. He had to use all his wife's money, and he eventually lost his positions in Stratford's government.

In Elizabethan times, everyone wore gloves—even indoors!

OFF TO SCHOOL

At about five years old, William went to his first school. At the time, only boys went to school. Girls were taught at home and learned how to sew and cook and keep house.

King's New School, Stratford.

At age seven, William went to King's New School in Stratford. He went to school six days a week. All lessons were taught in Latin, which was common in the 1500s. All the important jobs of the day—medicine, the Church, teaching, law, and politics—used Latin. The boys learned to read and write Latin using a **hornbook**. They also learned Greek, ancient history, and rhetoric, which was the art of making speeches. Every boy made his own quill pen by cutting the end off a goose feather.

Boys used hornbooks to practice reading and writing.

Actors in a scene from an updated modern-dress production of *As You Like It*.

A SOURCE OF STORIES

Among the subjects William studied were the works of ancient Roman writers such as Seneca and Ovid. Later, he used some of the stories he had learned at school as the basis for his plays. At the time, however, William may not have liked school. In his play *As You Like It*, he describes "the whining schoolboy, with his satchel, and shining morning face, creeping like a snail unwillingly to school." Schools were not free, but William's father did not have to pay because of his important job.

AFTER SCHOOL

William left school at age 14 or 15. Most young men from his background went on to university after school, but William did not. No one knows why. In November 1582, he married Anne Hathaway, the daughter of a wealthy landowner and farmer. William was only 18, but Anne was 26 years old. It was unusual for a man to marry at such a young age and to have a much older wife. The couple had three children. Susanna was born in 1583 and twins, Hamnet and Judith, in 1585.

THE LOST YEARS

Shakespeare experts call the period from 1585 to 1592 the "lost years." Nothing is known about what William did in the seven years after the birth of his twins. However, some people have come up with different theories about what William might have been doing during this time.

Anne Hathaway was eight years older than William.

William and his family relax at home in Stratford.

Using the plays as a starting point, some experts have suggested that William might have joined the army, because his plays are full of soldiers. Other experts say he worked in the law, because the plays show lots of legal knowledge. Another theory is that William was already working as an actor. We know that he was an actor when he was older, but in the 1580s several companies of actors visited Stratford to perform. In 1587, the Queen's Men, the leading acting company of the day, came to town. It could be that William not only watched the company but also joined them.

Elizabethan THEATER

Going to the theater was popular in Elizabethan times. However, the experience was not like going to the theater today.

When William was a boy, theaters were not special buildings. Companies of actors known as players performed outside in the yards of inns. The companies were all male. Men and boys played all the roles, even the roles of women. Players traveled from city to city to perform. By the time William moved to London in around 1587, however, London had a number of specially built theaters. The first, the Red Lion, opened in East London in 1567. It only lasted a few months. The first successful theater was also in East London. Built in 1576, it was simply called The Theater.

Theaters had very little scenery. The location of a scene was described in the words of the actors.

This cross-section of a theater shows the stage and the space for the audience.

Elizabethan theaters were built of wood. They were either round or six-sided. There was no roof, so if it rained the spectators and actors all got wet. Each playhouse had its own flag, which flew when there was a performance. Shows took place in daylight, because it was too dark at night. There was little scenery but lots of special effects. Angels and gods were lowered from the "heavens" and ghosts came up through a trapdoor. Actors supplied their own costumes.

Plays were classified as either **comedies** or **tragedies**. They were popular with all classes of people. The poorest spectators were the **groundlings**. They only paid a penny to enter—but they did not even get a seat. They stood in front of the stage. If they didn't like the show, they shouted and threw food at the actors!

Making a NAME

When William was in his mid-20s, he moved to London. He soon found success in the city's theatrical life.

Some time after 1587, William moved to London, England's capital city. The reasons why he left his wife and children in Stratford-upon-Avon and moved to London are unknown. For most of the next 20 years, he remained alone in the capital.

When William first arrived in London, it was the largest city not just in England but in the whole of northern Europe. A busy port, the city had grown up along the River Thames. It was a crowded, dirty city, full of all sorts of different people.

QUICK FACTS

- Theater was popular with everyone from rulers to the poor.
- Even so, some critics complained that it encouraged people to behave in an **immoral** way.

This drawing shows the Swan Theater on the south bank of the Thames River in London.

In 1600 London had 200,000 inhabitants, ten times more than any other city in England. London was the center of the law, the Church, and the economy. Trade made it wealthy. For a young man like William, it was an exciting place to live and work.

THE THEATER

Queen Elizabeth I often asked acting companies to perform for her in London. But many other people associated the theater with poor behavior among both the actors and the audience. These critics included the **guilds** who ran the City of London.

Meanwhile, **Puritans**, who followed a strict form of Christianity, condemned the theater as being immoral. Theaters were therefore built outside the City. Between 1567 and 1622, nine new theaters were built north and south of the Thames River.

Theaters were a profitable business. They were usually built by businessmen, who allowed a company of actors to perform and gave them a share of the profits. Unusually, The Theater was built by the actor James Burbage (1530–1597).

The Globe Theater stood in Bankside in London.

A NEW CAREER

When William arrived in London, the stage was dominated by a group of men nicknamed the "University Wits," because they had all studied at Oxford or Cambridge universities. They included Christopher Marlowe, Thomas Nashe, and Robert Greene. These playwrights wrote in a new style called **blank verse**, which used unrhymed lines, each of ten **syllables**. By 1592, William was also making a name for writing plays in blank verse.

How William came to write his first play is a mystery. Some historians believe he had joined a company of actors while he was still living in Stratford. William's early experience acting on stage probably helped him with his playwriting.

Christopher Marlowe was the leading playwright before Shakespeare appeared.

THE FIRST PLAYS

William wrote three plays about King Henry VI.

William may have started his dramatic career by rewriting other people's plays. No one knows for certain the name of his own first play. However, it may have been *Titus Andronicus* or *The Two Gentlemen of Verona*, written in around 1590. Between 1591 and 1593, William wrote successful history plays based on the stories of King Henry VI and Richard III. The other playwrights were jealous. Robert Greene attacked William, calling him an "upstart crow."

THE PLAGUE

William's new career came to a sudden halt when plague reached London in 1592. The disease spread through human contact. In order to stop it spreading, all London's theaters were closed after 30 people died from plague in a single week.

London during the plague.

The theaters did not open again until 1594. With no audience for any new plays, William turned to writing poems.

A POET

Poets were far more highly regarded than playwrights in Elizabethan England. William may have written poems earlier, but he did not publish any until 1593. He wrote mainly a form of poem called a sonnet. These 14-line poems dealt with emotions such as love. They are still popular today.

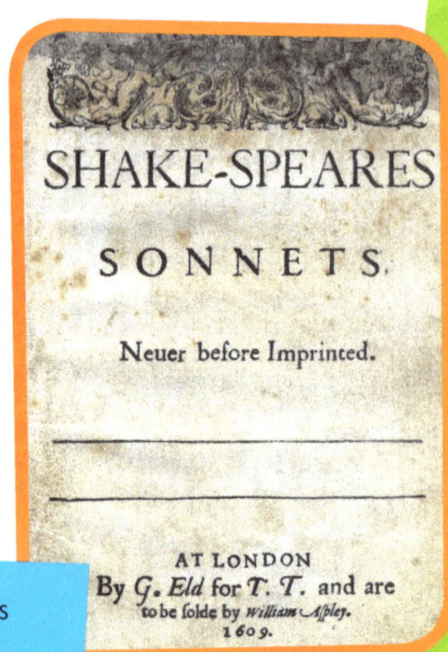
SHAKE-SPEARES

SONNETS.

Neuer before Imprinted.

AT LONDON
By G. Eld for T. T. and are
to be solde by William Aspley.
1609.

The first edition of William's sonnets, from 1609.

FAME

During the 1590s, William became increasingly famous. When the plague ended and the theaters reopened in 1594, William had found a rich **patron**, the Earl of Southampton. The earl's support brought William to the attention of Queen Elizabeth I. She invited William and other members of his acting company, the Lord Chamberlain's Men, to perform at her palace. William was soon a firm favorite of the queen.

Queen Elizabeth I.

By 1597, William had written some of his most famous plays, including *Romeo and Juliet*. The plays were so popular that he had become rich. He was able to send money back to Stratford to pay off his father's debts. Soon he was wealthy enough to buy his family a new home. William bought New Place, the second largest house in Stratford. However, tragedy also struck when William's son Hamnet died in 1596, at just 11 years old.

Life as an ACTOR

William Shakespeare worked as an actor before he started writing plays. At the time, the acting profession was not very glamorous.

In England in William's day, actors were always men. Acting was considered to be an immoral profession for women. Young men or boys played the female roles, such as Juliet. They wore a dress, wig, and makeup to look as much like a girl as possible. English travelers to other parts of Europe were amazed that women there acted on stage.

If you wanted to be an actor in Elizabethan England you had to join a company. A law passed in 1572 to deter **vagabonds** stated that any entertainer could be whipped unless he had a license to perform or was employed by a nobleman.

Like William, Edward Alleyn was a famous Elizabethan actor and businessman.

Scenery only appeared in the theater after William's death, as in this later performance of *King John*.

Companies of actors all had a patron. Shakespeare may have first joined the Earl of Worcester's company. It employed the best actor of the time, Edward Alleyn. He owned a number of theaters and organized bull and **bear-baiting** shows, which were very popular.

Actors rehearsed in the morning and performed in the afternoon. They performed many plays. If a play was unpopular, it was only performed once. If a play was popular, it was often copied by a rival company, who wrote down the words and then performed their own version.

Will Kemp was famous as a "clown," an actor who danced and sang.

A Series of GREAT PLAYS

Shakespeare's reputation continued to grow. In 1598, his name appeared for the first time on the title page of a play, *Love's Labours Lost*.

It was the first time his name had been printed on a play. William was so famous that his name guaranteed him success. But William was not only an actor and playwright, he was also a smart businessman. He and the rest of the Lord Chamberlain's Men acting company built a new theater, The Globe, on the south bank of the River Thames in 1599.

William had a 12.5 percent financial stake in the Globe, so he was entitled to a share of the ticket sales. Like other playhouses, the Globe was located just outside the City of London, so it was free from the City's strict rules.

QUICK FACTS

- William was smart enough to make sure he received a share of the earnings for his plays.
- It helped his popularity that he was the favorite of King James I!

In 1603, Queen Elizabeth I died. She had been a great supporter of William's career—but her successor and Scottish cousin, King James I, proved to be an even greater admirer of his work.

The new king granted the Lord Chamberlain's Men a **royal charter**. The document let the company rename themselves as the King's Men. It also allowed them to perform at court, at the Globe theater, and wherever else they wanted. Elizabeth I had wanted three performances a year, but James wanted the company to perform at court 13 times a year. That meant they needed a lot of new plays. William set out to provide them. They included some of his greatest plays, such as the tragedies *King Lear* and *Macbeth*.

A scene from *King Lear* in which the king talks to his daughter, Cordelia.

Hamlet meets the ghost of his father.

THE KING'S MAN

By this time, William was rich and famous. William's father, John, had died in 1601. However, he had lived to see his son restore the fortunes of the Shakespeare family.

In 1603, the year James I came to the English throne, plague hit London again. Around a quarter of the population died, and the theaters were closed again. The plague was not the only threat to the theater. James I wanted to keep the Puritans happy. He announced that there would be no more public theater performances on Sundays. This was a blow, because Sunday was traditionally the day most people went to the theater. The King's Men performed for James in his palaces outside London. William often played a small part in his own plays, such as the ghost in *Hamlet*.

Macbeth meets three witches who foretell his fate.

King James I was not formally crowned as king of England until 1604. William walked in the **coronation** procession through London. He was allowed to wear special red **livery** because of his service to the king. William was the first name on the list of actors who were allowed to wear red livery.

James I watched the King's Men perform eight of William's plays between Christmas 1604 and the following spring. They included *The Merry Wives of Windsor, Measure for Measure,* and *Love's Labours Lost*.

THE GREAT PLAYS

Between 1604 and 1608, William wrote most of his greatest tragedies. Some of the main roles were played by the actor Richard Burbage. He was the son of James Burbage, who had built The Theater in 1576. Richard played the title roles of *Othello*, *King Lear*, *Macbeth*, *Antony and Cleopatra*, and *Coriolanus*.

Macbeth is the story of a Scottish general who is told by three witches that he will become king. The prophecy comes true when Macbeth murders the real king, urged on by his wife, Lady Macbeth. Eventually he is defeated and overthrown.

William likely wrote the play in honor of James I. Before James became king of England, he had been king of Scotland. In addition, James had recently survived an **assassination** attempt on November 5, 1605, when Guy Fawkes and his fellow plotters attempted to blow up the Houses of Parliament.

The Gunpowder Plotters who tried to kill King James I.

This may be how the Blackfriars Theater looked inside.

ANOTHER NEW THEATER

In 1608, William's company took over a theater on the north bank of the River Thames at Blackfriars. Unlike earlier theaters, which had been open to the sky, the Blackfriars Theater was an indoor theater. It allowed the King's Men to perform during the winter. It was much smaller than the Globe, and attracted a different audience of courtiers and rich Londoners. The new audience wanted a different kind of play. Between 1608 and 1611, William wrote his late comedies, including *The Tempest*, for the new theater. With their fairy-tale plots and noble heroes and heroines, the plays were a big hit with the upmarket audience.

A RETURN TO STRATFORD

Sometime after 1611, when he had finished writing *The Tempest*, William left London. He returned to live with his family at New Place in Stratford-upon-Avon. His plays were still being performed, so he was still earning money, but he wanted to enjoy his retirement.

Musicians in a modern performance of a Shakespeare play at London's Globe Theatre.

Who Was SHAKESPEARE?

For a long time, people have wondered how someone with William's background could write such magnificent plays.

These critics argue that, because William came from a quiet country town and did not go to university, he could not have been educated enough to invent the phrases that appear in the plays. The critics wonder how, for example, William would have been able to write convincingly about places such as Venice and Verona in Italy when he had never traveled in Europe. Some people go so far as to say that William simply could not have written the plays alone. Over the centuries, experts have suggested a number of other authors who might have helped William, or even written the plays.

This balcony in the Italian city of Verona is said to be where Romeo visited Juliet.

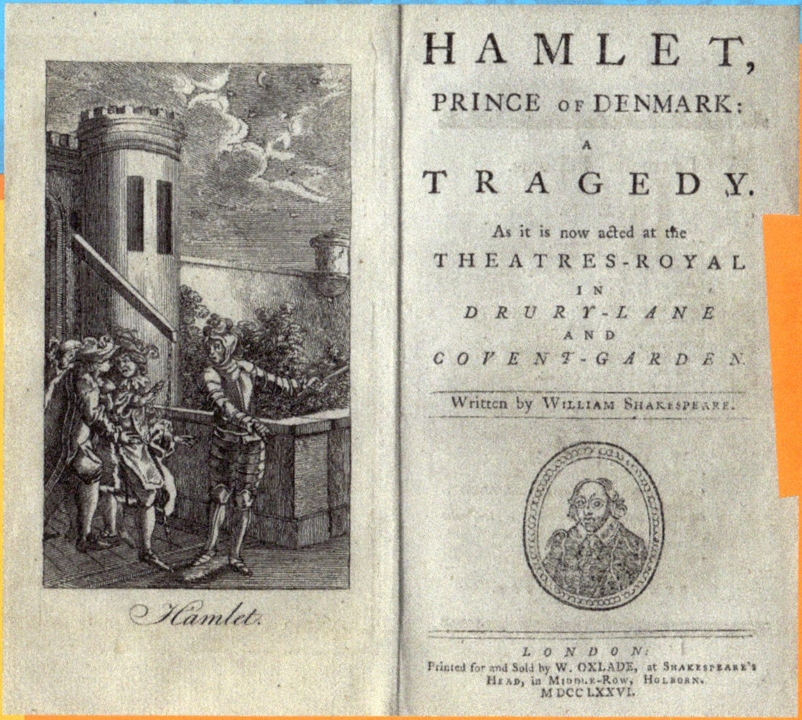
Hamlet.

HAMLET,
PRINCE OF DENMARK:
A
TRAGEDY.
As it is now acted at the
THEATRES-ROYAL
IN
DRURY-LANE
AND
COVENT-GARDEN.
Written by WILLIAM SHAKESPEARE.

LONDON:
Printed for and Sold by W. OXLADE, at SHAKESPEARE'S HEAD, in MIDDLE-ROW, HOLBORN.
MDCCLXXVI.

This is the first edition of *Hamlet*. Would William really have been able to write such a play?

A POSSIBLE CANDIDATE

One popular suggestion is that the plays were written by Edward de Vere, the 17th Earl of Oxford. His supporters say that he had the education, experience, and social status that would have enabled him to write such plays. Yet de Vere died in 1604, before 15 of the plays were written.

Edward de Vere was a leading noble of the time.

No evidence has been produced to show that William did not write the plays. Today, most experts are convinced that he was indeed the author, however unlikely that might seem.

A Lasting REPUTATION

More than 400 years after William's death, people are still fascinated by the man, the times he lived in, and the plays he wrote.

When William returned to live with his family in Stratford, he was a rich and successful man. But although he lived in comfort in New Place, he continued to visit London regularly. He wanted to look after his business interests at the Globe Theater. Shakespeare had given up acting and no longer wrote his own plays, but he still **collaborated** on plays with younger playwrights. The dramatist he worked with most was John Fletcher, who wrote many plays for William's former acting company, the King's Men.

QUICK FACTS

- Different versions exist of some of William's plays.
- The plays were not all collected and published together until after his death!

After 1613, there is no record of any more plays by Shakespeare. On June 29, a cannon was fired during a production of *Henry VIII* at the Globe Theater. The cannon set fire to the theater's straw roof. In less than an hour, the Globe burned down. The accident may have made William decide to give up the theater and finally retire.

A stage cannon burned down the first Globe Theater.

THE CURTAIN FALLS

In April 1616, the playwright Ben Jonson visited his friend William in Stratford. They were later joined by the poet Michael Drayton, who lived close by. The friends ate some pickled herrings and drank wine.

Ben Jonson called his evening with William "a merrie meeting."

Soon after the meeting, William fell ill. Only in March, he had signed a will in which he declared himself fit and healthy. Less than a month later, on his given birthday, April 23, 1616, William Shakespeare died at the age of 52.

William was buried two days later in Holy Trinity Church in Stratford. The church register entered his death as "Will. Shakespeare, gent." On his tomb was carved a warning: "Good friend, for Jesus' sake forbear, / To dig the dust enclosed here. / Blessed be the man that spares these stones, / And cursed be he that moves my bones."

This monument to William Shakespeare is in Westminster Abbey in London.

William left most of his property to his older daughter, Susanna. To his wife, Anne Hathaway, he left "the second-best bed." For centuries, people have wondered whether this was an insult or a kind gift. Why did Anne not receive the best bed? William also remembered his actor friends. He left Richard Burbage enough money to buy himself a ring to wear in William's memory.

PUBLISHED WORKS

During William's life, only half of his plays were published. They appeared in quartos. Quartos were made using sheets of paper that had been folded twice to make four leaves, or eight pages. The quartos were published without William's permission, so he did not get to see the text. These **pirated** copies contained many mistakes and lines that William almost certainly did not actually write.

Beds were valuable pieces of furniture in William's time.

A scene from *A Midsummer Night's Dream.*

In 1623, two of William's friends decided it was time to stop inaccurate copies of his plays being printed. John Heminge and Henry Condell were members of the King's Men. They collected the texts of 36 of William's plays, 18 of which had never been published (another had been lost). The two men published the plays in a collection called the First Folio. They wanted the book "to keep the memory of so worthy a friend and fellow alive."

Heminge and Condell also included a portrait of William. People said at the time it was a good likeness, which is why we have some idea of what William looked like. The plays in the First Folio sometimes differed **radically** from those in the previous quartos. For example, the two versions of *King Lear* are completely different. The Folio edition is considered by experts to be the **authoritative** version.

MR. WILLIAM
SHAKESPEARES
COMEDIES,
HISTORIES, &
TRAGEDIES.
Published according to the True Originall Copies.

LONDON
Printed by Isaac Iaggard, and Ed. Blount. 1623.

William's portrait in the First Folio.

WILLIAM'S LEGACY

Four centuries after William died, his works are still studied by students everywhere. He is the most performed playwright in the world. His plays are translated in many languages. Tourists still flock to Stratford-upon-Avon to watch plays at the Swan Theater. In London, the Globe Theater was rebuilt on its original site in 1997.

The Globe Theater in London.

The Swan Theater in Stratford-upon-Avon.

The Globe puts on traditional versions of William's plays. Modern theatergoers can stand in front of the stage and experience a play as "groundlings!"

WILLIAM'S LANGUAGE

Although it is 400 years since William died, his language often seems very modern. William used more words in his plays than any other writer in English. He also made up words and phrases. Many of these phrases are now in common use in English: "quick as a flash," "cold comfort," and "good riddance" are phrases created by William. You may even have quoted William if you have ever said, for example, "I have not slept one wink" (*Cymbeline*) or "It was all Greek to me" (*Julius Caesar*). Because such phrases are so popular, they continue to keep William's work alive.

Timeline

1564 · c. April 23: born in Stratford upon Avon. He is baptized on April 26.

1568-69 · Wiliam's father, John, holds positions on the town council in Stratford.

1576 · The Theater opens in London.

1582 · c. November 28: Wiliam Marries Anne Hathaway.

1583 · Anne gives birth to a daughter, Susanna.

1585 · Birth of twins, Judith and Hamnet.

1587 · Possible year William moves to London.

1592 · Robert Greene calls William an "upstart crow."

1592-3 · Plague closes London's theaters.

1593 · William publishes his first poem, "Venus and Adonis."

1594 · *The Comedy of Errors* is performed at London's Gray's Inn.

1595 · William becomes a member of the Lord Chamberlain's Men, who perform at court.

1596 · Hamnet Shakespeare dies.

1597 · William buys New Place in Stratford.

1599 · The Globe Theater opens on London's Bankside.

1601 · John Shakespeare dies.
· The Lord Chamberlain's men perform *Richard II* at the Globe.

1603	· Queen Elizabeth I dies. · James VI of Scotland becomes James I of England. · The Lord Chamberlain's Men become the King's Men.
1604	· At least five of William's plays are performed at court.
1605	· The Gunpowder Plot fails to blow up the king and the English parliament. Shakespeare writes *Macbeth*.
1609	· King's Men perform at Blackfriars Theater.
1611-12	· *The Tempest* and *The Winter's Tale* are performed at court. · Leaves London for Stratford after 1611.
1613	· The Globe burns down.
1616	· April 23: Dies in Stratford.
1623	· First Folio published.

KEY PLAYS AND APPROXIMATE DATES

- *Romeo and Juliet* (1595)
- *A Midsummer Night's Dream* (1595)
- *Henry IV, Part 1* (1596-1597)
- *The Merchant of Venice* (1596-1597)
- *Hamlet* (1599-1601)
- *Othello* (1603-1604)
- *King Lear* (1605-1606)
- *Macbeth* (1606)
- *Antony and Cleopatra* (1606)
- *The Tempest* (1610-1611)

Glossary

assassination A murder committed for a political reason.

authoritative Trusted as being true and accurate.

bear-baiting An entertainment in which dogs attacked a captive bear.

blank verse A form of verse that usually has ten syllables a line, and which does not rhyme.

collaborated Worked together with someone on a project.

comedies Plays that have relatively lighthearted messages.

coronation A ceremony in which a monarch is crowned.

groundlings Theatergoers who stood in front of the stage.

guilds Trade organizations.

hornbook A tablet with the letters of the alphabet.

immoral Sinful or evil.

livery A special uniform worn by the servants of a noble.

patron A person who supports an individual or organization.

patron saint The saint said to protect a place.

pirated Copied and sold without permission.

plague A deadly disease.

playwright Someone who writes plays.

Puritans Followers of a strict form of Protestantism.

radically In a far-reaching and thorough way.

royal charter A document granting special privileges from a king or queen.

sonnets Rhyming poems of 14 lines, often dealing with emotions.

syllables The separate parts of sound in a word.

tragedies Plays in which a noble hero comes to a fatal end because of a character flaw.

vagabonds Hoboes or tramps.

Further Resources

Books

Berne, Emma Carlson. *William Shakespeare: Playwright and Poet.* Essential Lives. Edina, Minn.: ABDO Publishing Co., 2008.

DK Eyewitness Books. *Shakespeare.* New York: Dorling Kindersley, 2015.

Kuiper, Kathleen. *The Life and Times of William Shakespeare.* Shakespeare: His Work and World. New York: Rosen Publishing, 2012.

Mannis, Celeste Davidson. *Who Was William Shakespeare?* Who Was? New York: Grosset and Dunlap, 2007.

Nettleton, Pamela Hill. *William Shakespeare: The Inspiring Life Story of the Playwright Extraordinaire.* Inspiring Stories. North Mankato, Minn: Compass Point Books, 2017.

Raum, Elizabeth. *Twenty-First Century Shakespeare.* Culture in Action. Chicago, Ill: Raintree, 2010.

Websites

BBC History
www.bbc.co.uk/schools/primaryhistory/famouspeople/william_shakespeare/
A detailed timeline of William Shakespeare's life.

Biography.com
www.biography.com/people/william-shakespeare-9480323
A biography and video about Shakespeare's life.

DK Find Out!
www.dkfindout.com/uk/music-art-and-literature/shakespeares-globe/william-shakespeare/
A biography of Shakespeare with many links.

Ducksters
www.ducksters.com/biography/authors/william_shakespeare.php
A biography of Shakespeare.

Index